WOODPECKER WHAM!

For Jeff
and all the woodpeckers we've watched
and all the trees that held them
—A. P. S.

For April
—S. J.

Henry Holt and Company, LLC
Publishers since 1866
175 Fifth Avenue
New York, New York 10010
mackids.com

Henry Holt® is a registered trademark of Henry Holt and Company, LLC.
Text copyright © 2015 by April Pulley Sayre
Illustrations copyright © 2015 by Steve Jenkins

Library of Congress Cataloging-in-Publication Data
Sayre, April Pulley, author.
Woodpecker wham! / April Pulley Sayre ; illustrated by Steve Jenkins. — First edition.
pages   cm
Audience: Ages 4–8.
Includes bibliographical references.
ISBN 978-0-8050-8842-7 (hardcover)
1. Woodpeckers—Behavior—Juvenile literature. 2. Woodpeckers—Juvenile literature.
I. Jenkins, Steve, 1952– illustrator. II. Title.
QL696.P56S384 2015   598.7'2—dc23   2014038047

Henry Holt books may be purchased for business or promotional use. For information on bulk purchases,
please contact the Macmillan Corporate and Premium Sales Department at (800) 221-7945 x5442
or by e-mail at specialmarkets@macmillan.com.

First Edition—2015/Designed by Ashley Halsey
The artist used cut- and torn-paper collage to create the illustrations for this book.
Printed in China by South China Printing Co. Ltd., Dongguan City, Guangdong Province

1 3 5 7 9 10 8 6 4 2

WOODPECKER WHAM!

April Pulley Sayre

Illustrated by **Steve Jenkins**

Henry Holt and Company
New York

Swoop and land.
Hitch and hop.
Shred a tree stump.
CHOP, CHIP, CHOP!

Instant message.
Tap—one, two!
BONK-BONK-BONK.
Now back to you!

Early insects
click and crawl.
Flick and flake
to find them all.

Spring sap rises.
Who will drill?
Sapsucker, sapsucker,
sticky bill!

Fan those feathers.
Shower clean.
Sunbathe dry.
Then oil and preen!

Raise that crest.
Bob and bow.
Flash those wings.
It's time to wow!

Start a home.
Bill to bark.
Dig it, dig it—
deep and dark.

Wedge it. Sledge it.
Wham by wham.
Clear those chips.
SLAM, SLAM, SLAM!

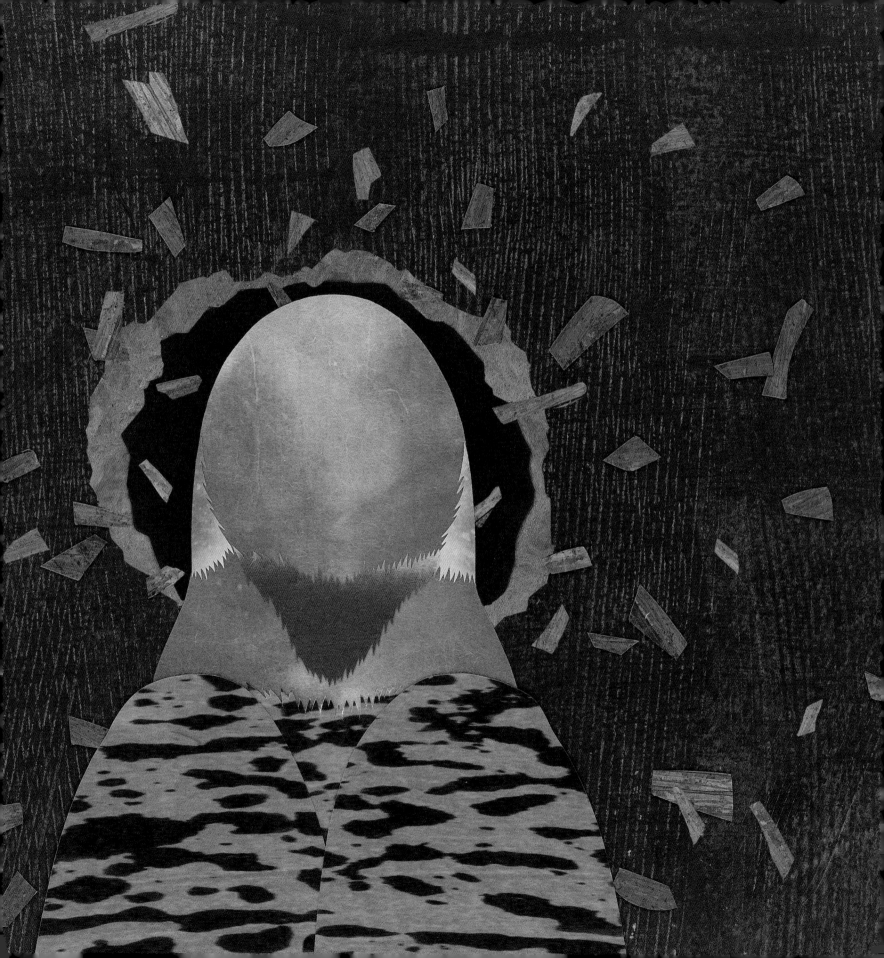

Hawk's a-hunting.
Stop. Drop. Hide.
Quiet
on the other side.

Cherries, berries.
Pluck and feed.
Leave a dropping
full of seed.

TAP, TAP, TAP.
Where? Look and see.
CRICK, CRICK, CRACK!
Six chicks break free.

Hungry mouths and
begging calls.
Hunt, hop, pick.
Quick! Feed them all!

Fledglings fly. Oops!
Fledglings flop.
Chase and feed.
When will it stop?

Fluffy fledglings
now are grown.
WIK-A, WIK-A!
On their own.

Fall is falling.
Acorns plunk.
Pry seeds. Pull seeds.
Fill a trunk!

Leave that tree hole.
Start one new.
Who will move in
after you?

Bill to bark. Build!
SLAM, SLAM, SLAM!
Chip and chop.
Woodpecker **WHAM!**

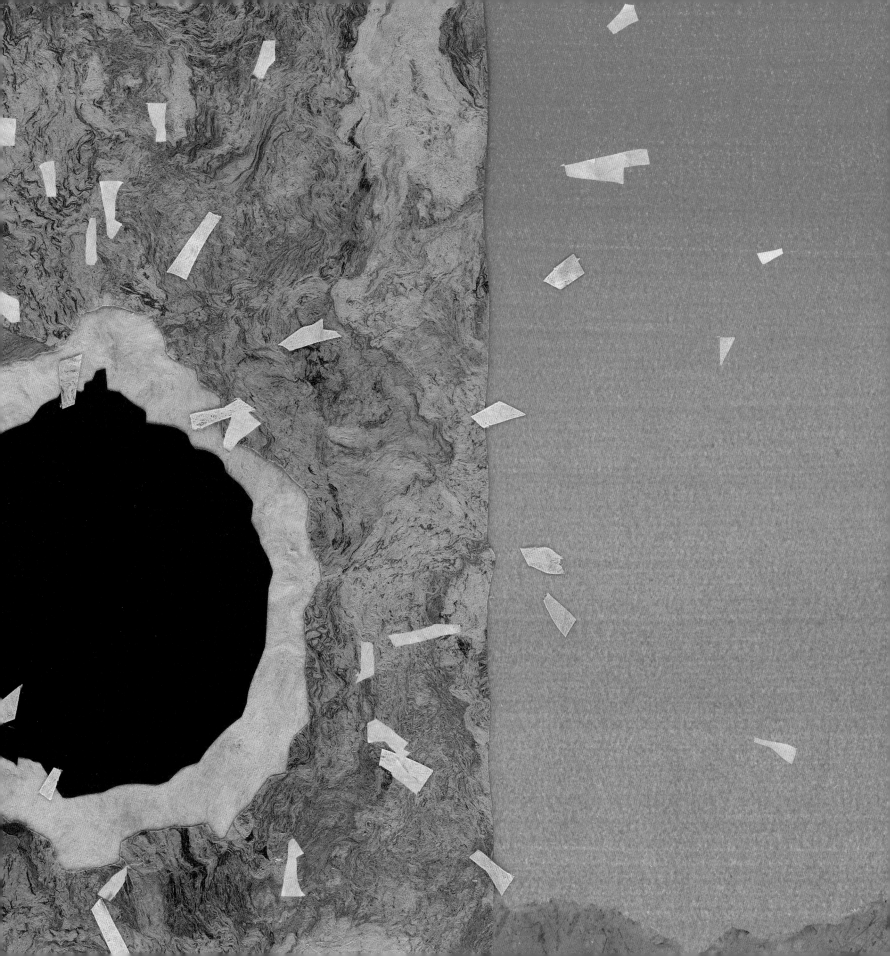

WOODPECKER WORLD

Champion Chiselers

To chisel wood, woodpeckers have big, strong bills with wedge-like or chisel-like tips. Feather tufts cover their nostrils to keep wood flakes out as they dig. In Mexico, people call woodpeckers *pájaros carpinteros*, meaning "carpenter birds."

Hitch and Hop

When clinging to bark, a woodpecker hangs on with its hooked claws. Its stiff tail helps to prop up its body. To travel up a tree, a woodpecker lets go for a moment and hops forward with both feet. The hop happens so quickly, it's hard to see. This action is called hitching.

Instant Messages

Woodpeckers tap, or drum, to make noise. Often they have favorite drumming sites: dead trees, hollow branches, chimney caps—any place that amplifies the sound. Both males and females drum, but males drum louder and more often. Drumming and calling help a woodpecker attract a mate, claim a territory, or just keep in touch. (It's like saying "Where are you?" and answering "I'm over here!")

Woodpecker Tongues

A woodpecker's tongue is so long and flexible that it can snake into a beetle tunnel underneath a tree's bark. In the center of a woodpecker's tongue is the hyoid apparatus, a thin, bony structure that branches and wraps around the back of the bird's skull. The muscles of the tongue are attached to it. The hyoid slides forward and backward as the tongue extends and retracts.

Most woodpecker tongues are pointed and barbed at the tip. Others have bristles like pipe cleaners or brushes that soak up tree sap. All woodpeckers have sticky saliva that helps them grab prey and hold on to food.

But how do woodpeckers know where to dig? First the woodpecker taps the tree. This causes insects inside to move. The woodpecker hears the movement or feels the vibrations through its bill. Then it flakes off more bark or digs deeper to reach the termites, ants, beetles, or grubs—soft, plump insect larvae.

Pileated woodpecker

Sap: A Sticky Business

Underneath tree bark are channels where sweet sap runs. To reach this food, sapsuckers dig small, shallow holes called sap wells. Sap oozes out, and the sapsucker licks it up with its bristled tongue. It also eats any insects that get caught in the sticky sap.

Nuthatches, warblers, hummingbirds, chipmunks, squirrels, porcupines, and even bats eat the sap that seeps into woodpecker-drilled tree holes. As the sap dries, it hardens, closing the hole. The woodpecker must return and "tap" the trees again to reopen the holes. (Of course, wild animals aren't the only sap eaters. Humans boil down maple tree sap to concentrate its sugars and make maple syrup!)

Seeds by Splat

Many woodpeckers eat cherries, blackberries, and other small fruits. If the seeds are eaten along with the fruit, they can travel through a bird's body unharmed and end up in its droppings—and wherever those land, a plant may grow. The rest of the droppings can help fertilize the new plants.

Nutty Foods

Woodpeckers eat bigger seeds as well, including acorns, beechnuts, and almonds. Often a woodpecker will grab a nut, fly to a tree, and wedge it into a crevice in the bark. It slams its bill on the seed to crack it open.

Red-headed woodpecker

The acorn woodpecker, which lives in the western United States, is famous for chiseling acorn-sized holes in dead trees and jamming an acorn into each hole. Families of acorn woodpeckers carefully defend these acorn stashes, called granaries.

Red-headed woodpeckers, which live in the eastern United States, store acorns too, but not on the grand scale that acorn woodpeckers do. Red-headed woodpeckers stash them in piles inside hollow branches and tree trunks.

Getting Along

Many kinds of woodpeckers can live peacefully in one forest. How? Because, for the most part, they do not compete for food. Some eat sap. Some specialize in eating acorns. Others eat mostly insects. Or they may eat the same foods but hunt for them in different ways or places. For instance, some woodpeckers dig shallow pits to find insects; others dig deep into

Downy woodpecker

rotting wood. Some woodpeckers hunt insects close to the ground, while others hunt high up in the trees. All the woodpeckers shown in this book live together in eastern deciduous forests of the United States. (Some of these same species range into the western United States as well.)

Woodpecker Feeders

To attract wild woodpeckers, many people put out birdfeeders containing sunflower seeds, peanuts, or suet. Suet is animal fat, and it gives the birds some of the nutrients they would otherwise gain from eating insects and spiders. (Downy woodpeckers have been seen picking at animal carcasses in winter, so fat is a natural winter food for them.) Woodpeckers may also sip from hummingbird feeders, which are filled with sugar water. Some woodpeckers eat bananas or oranges set out on a feeder.

Cleanup Time

To clean their feathers, woodpeckers flutter them in rain and against wet leaves. They sunbathe to warm and dry their feathers. They preen, using their bills to pick out dirt and straighten their feathers. They also take dust baths. Sifting dust through their feathers helps get rid of grime and mites. In winter, downy woodpeckers may take snow baths. A downy ducks its head and neck into the snow and flings snow over its back.

Anting

Woodpeckers occasionally "ant." That is, they sit on an anthill and let ants crawl over their body. Or they grasp an ant in their bill and rub it over their feathers. Scientists are not sure why birds do this. It's possible that the formic acid ants spray in defense helps rid the birds' feathers of mites and other biting creatures.

Raising a Family

Most female woodpeckers lay approximately three to six eggs in each clutch, or batch, of eggs. The parents keep the eggs warm by sitting on them. An incubation patch (a featherless area of skin on the parents' bellies) helps them use their body heat to warm the eggs. In about two weeks, the eggs hatch. Newly hatched woodpeckers are featherless, and their eyes are closed. The male and female share the work of caring for the eggs and chicks.

Feeding Time

For up to a month, woodpecker parents care for their chicks. They may bring them whole insects. Or they may swallow food, take it to the nest, then regurgitate it—cough it up into the chicks' mouths. (That way the food is soft and portable, and it's easier for the chicks to digest.) In a few weeks, the chicks take their first flight. Once out of the nesting cavity, they are unlikely to return. But the adults find the chicks and feed them for several days or weeks.

Barklike Bodies

Bars, spots, or streaks are common color patterns for woodpeckers. These marks probably act as camouflage to help them blend in with the background, which is often tree bark. Male and female woodpeckers generally look similar. The male may have red or yellow marks on his head—or both the male and female may have these marks, but the male will have larger ones. Some males have a red or black "malar stripe" across the cheek area. Young woodpeckers, in most cases, appear duller in color than the adults. Young red-headed woodpeckers are brown and white, not the bright red color of the adults.

Drilling for Cavities

Most woodpeckers live in holes called cavities. These may be in living trees, dead trees, stumps, fence posts, cacti, or even riverbanks. Both males and females may help dig out these holes, and there are two different types: roosting cavities and nesting cavities. Roosting cavities are where woodpeckers rest and sleep when they are not caring for eggs or chicks in the nest. Nesting cavities are where woodpeckers lay their eggs and raise their young. A woodpecker cavity can take from a week to many months or more to excavate. (The red-cockaded woodpecker can take over four years to finish digging its home in a live pine tree.) Woodpeckers may work steadily on the project or only intermittently.

Home Security

To make its nesting cavity, a woodpecker usually digs straight into the wood. Then it tunnels downward to hollow out a large nesting chamber.

Yellow-bellied sapsucker

This curved entrance likely makes it harder for raccoons and other predators to reach the eggs or young.

Woodpeckers: Home Builders

Many animals use natural holes in trees. But woodpeckers are among the only creatures equipped to carve out new ones. After a woodpecker abandons a nesting cavity, squirrels, raccoons, nuthatches, wrens, ducks, owls, bats, bees, or other animals may move in. Biologists call many types of woodpeckers "keystone" species because their holes provide nest sites that are critical to the survival of other species.

Helping Woodpeckers

The best way to attract woodpeckers is to provide their overall habitat. Plant bushes, trees, and cacti that supply fruits and nuts. (Woodpeckers eat the fruit of the prickly pear cactus, for instance.) Preserve large trees where

Northern flicker

woodpeckers could nest. Snags—dead trees—should be left standing when possible. Even if the top of a tree must be cut, leaving a tall section of the trunk can provide a home for woodpeckers, owls, and other wildlife. Don't forget to plant some trees that grow big enough to create nesting holes. These may take decades to grow to the size a woodpecker needs. But planting them will help future woodpeckers and future woodpecker fans.

How to Find a Woodpecker

Woodpeckers belong to one of the most widespread bird families, with more than two hundred species worldwide. So if you have trees or large cacti nearby, you have a good chance of seeing one.

- Look for medium-size birds. The smallest woodpeckers are piculets, which live in tropical areas and can be as tiny as three inches (7.6 centimeters) long. The largest woodpecker is the 22-inch (56-centimeter) imperial woodpecker of Mexico, the size of a red-tailed hawk. But you're not likely to see that one. Scientists have not seen any imperial woodpeckers in several decades, and the species could be extinct. You may, however, see the more widespread pileated woodpecker, which is still huge, at 16 to 19 inches (41 to 48 centimeters) long!

- Listen for drumming—the sound of tapping on trees or cacti.

- Look for large trees or cacti. Examine tree trunks for rows of holes or patches bare of bark. If you see these signs, a woodpecker may have been excavating to find insects, drilling for tree sap, or building a home. (Note that some other animals, such as bears and porcupines, also pull bark off trees.)

- Keep an eye out for wood chips on the ground. They could be from a woodpecker digging holes high above.

- Look for birds with a flap-and-glide flight pattern. Most woodpeckers flap their wings, then pause as they lose altitude, then flap their wings again. This intermittent flight makes them undulate, or rise and fall noticeably, as they fly.

- In the desert, look for a "saguaro boot." When a Gila woodpecker digs a home in a saguaro cactus, the cactus heals by hardening the area around the nesting cavity. Long after the rest of the cactus has rotted, the old nesting cavities, usually boot-shaped, remain. If you see them lying around, you'll know that woodpeckers have been in the area.

- Take a winter walk. Most woodpeckers do not migrate—journey long distances regularly—in spring and fall, as many other birds do. (Yellow-bellied sapsuckers and northern flickers are exceptions.) So even when the snow is falling, northern birdwatchers may hear woodpeckers calling or tapping on trees. It can be easier to see woodpeckers in winter, when many of the trees have shed their leaves.

Red-bellied woodpecker

Further Reading

Cate, Annette LeBlanc. *Look Up! Bird-Watching in Your Own Backyard*. Somerville, MA: Candlewick, 2013.

Davies, Jacqueline, and Melissa Sweet. *The Boy Who Drew Birds: A Story of John James Audubon*. Boston: Houghton Mifflin Co., 2004.

Lasky, Kathryn, and David Catrow. *She's Wearing a Dead Bird on Her Head!* New York: Hyperion Books for Children, 1995.

Sayre, April Pulley. *Touch a Butterfly: Wildlife Gardening with Kids*. Boston: Roost Books, 2013.

Sayre, April Pulley, and Gary Locke. *Bird, Bird, Bird! (A Chirping Chant)*. Minnetonka, MN: NorthWord Books for Young Readers, 2007.

For more about woodpecker species, type "woodpeckers" in the search box of the Cornell Lab of Ornithology's "All About Birds" website (allaboutbirds.org).

Young researchers who want to dig deeper will find scholarly yet readable life histories of all North American birds, including woodpecker species, on the Birds of North America online site (bna.birds.cornell.edu/bna).

AUTHOR'S ACKNOWLEDGMENTS

Thank you to woodpecker biologist Jerome A. Jackson of the Department of Marine and Ecological Sciences at Florida Gulf Coast University. Thanks also to Dr. Lester L. Short, Cornell Lab of Ornithology, and Bill Evans. Gratitude to Mom, JoAnn Early Macken, Carmela Martino, Gretchen Woelfle, Donnie and Andrea Rogers, and an anonymous tree company climber who was a huge help during a woodpecker crisis.